AF264583

Single MOTHERS *for the* Win

Written by: Andrea J. Watson

ISBN: 978-0-578-67407-0

DEDICATION

This book is dedicated to my sons, Keith Jr., and Kevin. As of now, you have no idea how much I struggle, but years from now when you are grown you can see how I did it in the details of this book.

CONTENTS

ACKNOWLEDGMENTS

Mom, I acknowledge you. Thank you for shaping me into the woman I am today. With the little time you have on this earth, you did a phenomenal job.

Thank you, G-mama and G-daddy, for taking me and my boys underneath your wings. Y'all were truly sent from heaven.

To all the single mothers whose stories went untold, you hold a special place in my heart every day.

1

Acceptance

Yes, this is my first book, and I am so excited. Hopefully, you are a single mother. If you are not, cool, but this isn't a book on how to raise your kids because I would never tell any woman how to do that. No one can. This is not a baby-daddy bashing book, either This book is for those who aspire to more than being a single mother. Yes, that is your current situation, but those who know that your life has been called for a purpose and are trying to navigate in the midst of the children, you are the ones who are trying to level up and don't know where to begin, it's OK, sis. I got you. I thank you for choosing this book to read.

Let's begin with the fact that no matter where you are on the spectrum from struggling and living paycheck to paycheck to thriving and working in a multimillion-dollar corporation, let's agree you're not just here to struggle, pay bills, and die. You have a purpose, and you have baby humans to raise who depend on you for every need. The first step in understating this is acceptance. As a woman, you bear the primary responsibility of the children, point-blank, period. You can't blame anyone else for getting pregnant but yourself; that's just the society we live in.

It just is what it is. I found it easier to accept the fact that I was a single mother. It made no sense for me to be in denial, complain, or be bitter and question my circumstance: Why me? Why this lifestyle? What did I do wrong? Why he won't take care of the kids? Blah, blah, blah. To hell with it all. Seriously, you will drive yourself crazy trying to make it make sense, so just let it be. Let it go!

The truth is you had kids by a man, and it didn't work out, so you left him, or a harder truth is you had a baby by a man who left you and your child because he wanted to. There is no law to say that a man must stay with you because you had his baby. The real issue is how an absentee father is going to impact your relationship with your child.

As a single mother, I would never try to make up for the absent father or overcompensate. My thought is if the father is not available for your child emotionally, physically, mentally, or financially, my friend, you are a single mother. Do the best you can with the natural skill you have. I've seen other women live miserable lives having a boyfriend and still complaining about how much needs to be done for the family. The crazy part about that is that you can sleep with a man or have a live-in man, but if he does not engage with your kids with the ways I listed above, you are still a single mother.

I did not want to be that type of mother. I'd rather be by myself with peace of mind. I noticed that with peace of mind, as a single mother, you have the power to create the lifestyle you want for your kids. Dream big; that's what I did. Also, take the time to come up with a vision for your lifestyle; dream about how you want your daily life to be with your kids. Don't get lost, whatever your current situation is. One thing about hardships is that they are temporary. Always remember, it's not where you have been, it's where you are going. Keep pressing forward. That's what's life is about: its creation.

Whatever your vision is, you have the full capability to do that and gain victories along the way, such as finishing school, fixing your credit, or starting a business. Create your lifestyle, ladies; it's all up for grabs. You can make your lifestyle as high or low maintenance as you want. You want a mansion and to live lavishly? Be my guest. You want a beach house so that your kids can play in the sand all day? Yep, you can do that too. How about a country farmhouse so the babies can run through the acres? Just imagine that.

This is not a book to tell you how to raise your kids or baby-daddy bash but to let you know just because you are single, voids shouldn't be missing from your and your kids' life. Whether business, finance, or social, you should have no voids. My aim is that at the end of this book, you will feel empowered as a single mother to live a life doing what you want. When you feel like you are stuck, don't stay there; learn how to turn that feeling into the change you want to see. Even if you can't move right now and leave the city for whatever reason, you must learn to make the best of the situation. Something good will come from it. Basically, do what you need to do to have peace of mind knowing you are doing all that you have to in order to live comfortably.

I refused to raise my kids as a fourth-generation below the poverty line. I decided to uproot my kids and relocate so I could provide a better life for them as a single mother. Sometimes you must just make the move.

I could have stayed in my comfort zone in San Diego, room-mating and living with family members, but that was not the lifestyle I wanted. So, I planned to escape. But first I had to figure out where I was going to live, so I did some research.

I visited some places to live in Northern California, Las Vegas, Phoenix, Dallas, Houston, and Austin, Texas. Keep in mind as I was researching cities and states, I was looking into school systems, crime rates, and the price of living because I wanted a change. The city and state that completed my checklist was Austin, Texas. It had blue-ribbon schools, the crime rate was low, and the price of living was affordable. Without hesitation I knew the vibe was right. I was confident in my decision.

I applied for work with whatever working experience I could remember from customer service, health care, and retail. I just had to get in somewhere to plant my seed. I was submitting my resume to any job search for which I had skills and experience. This part was aggressive. If I could put a number to it, then I was submitting about twenty applications a day. Then I would find the hiring manager or company's recruiter to email or make a follow-up call to check the status of my resume. The follow-up is key in any job search because most people don't even bother if it's an electronic email, but you can always look up whoever is in charge of HR and email them personally. You see, when you have a laser-focused vision, you will do what you must to make your vision come to pass. Even if I had to go out of my way, I was willing to invest in going the extra mile. I was on a mission to get a job and would not stop until my mission was accomplished.

During this time, I had set a tight budget because it was only me with one source of income at the time. It was fine at that moment because that was all I needed. It was going to take self-control to save what I needed, but I stayed focused on my vision to get me through. I cut out every expense possible. I only bought what I needed, not what I wanted, but I will talk about that in the next chapter. I was in transition to moving out of state. I left my apartment to move in with a friend's family. I told myself that this was going to be the *last time* I would ever live with someone, and that was my motivation to save. I told my childhood best friend and my mother the situation about how I was in the process of moving I needed about six months to stay with them so I could save money and create a new life. They said yes.

It was a huge relief to know that I had some support. Other women might not be so fortunate. I was thankful for the opportunity. My two kids and I shared a room, slept in the same bed, and kept to ourselves as I was planning for our new life. I was working out, eating clean, practicing mediations, and saving everything. I barely went out except to work and home.

In the midst of it all, I was still applying for work during those six months. The medical laboratory job I applied to called me about a position similar to what I was currently doing in the A/R department, and they were interested in interviewing me. I told them my situation that I was relocating, and I requested a Skype interview. I knew that I was not going to fly out for every interview I could get.

Ladies, when you are in transition, you cannot settle because that defeats the purpose; you have to set standards. This is only the beginning.

Communication is key. I asked for what I needed to accept the position. I asked the hiring manager for higher pay and an offer letter with a start date with a two-weeks' time because I was moving from another state, and I still needed a place to stay. This happened after the interview was completed, you can have open communication, and some employers will work with you.

In the meantime, I was looking for an apartment. I wanted nothing fancy to begin with; all I needed was a one-bedroom, one-bath close to a school for the boys and a light commute to and from work. Thank the Lord for Google Maps; it was a lifesaver. I could see the distance from work, home, and the boys' school, and I loved that. I found my place. I knew what I wanted, and I was not going to settle until I got it.

Many people have asked me if I just up and moved to another state because I gave off that illusion, but I did not, and I would not recommend that. As a single mother, you do not move out of state without a job offer in writing and a place to stay as a bare minimum. It's called safekeeping.

After I called the apartment I was interested in, I applied online, signed my paperwork, and paid my deposit so when I arrived within the next two days, all I had to do was get my keys and move in. It was the best feeling ever; I'm glad I planned it that way. I may make it sound easy, but it took eighteen months of preparation to plan my life-changing decision. Every day, I woke up saying, "I'm one day closer to leaving San Diego." If you are debating leaving your hometown, make the move. If you are terrified, make the move anyway. Accept it!

2

Budget & finance

When it comes to money, it's never about how much money you make but how much you spend. That's why I am a huge advocate of saving. And the secret to that is living below your means. I'm not the type of person to count anyone's pockets or judge them for making money or the lack thereof. Nobody ever taught me the concepts of saving money; however, I did learn that most people don't really have a money issue. They have a debt/spending issue. So, you must do what is needed to eliminate it. Pay off all debt if that's the problem. Debt is financial cancer; it will eat you alive financially, and you won't be able to save money and see the fruits of your labor if you have debt. Some tips to eliminate debt are to work extra hours but who really wants to do that? Pick up a part-time job, start an online business, sell a product to generate some income, and stop overspending.

I learned overspending comes from a poverty mindset, feeling like you do not have enough or are not getting your needs met. While I was growing up, my mother used to shop like the world was about to end, and I never understood it until I learned it was her mindset of, "I have to get this now, or it won't be here later."

Unfortunately, I developed that habit as well. I had to teach myself that when I shop, I only get what I need at the current moment. I don't need to buy everything in double quantity. I was doing that out of habit. Now I put any extra funds toward paying off debt. You have the control to tell where your money goes. Every time you get paid and all expenses have been paid, even if it's only $5 left in your checking account, transfer it to pay debt. The quicker you pay debt back the better.

Start to teach you kids about money and finances at a young age so they won't make the same mistakes. Break the generational curse of poverty in your family, and teach yourself how to become a money magnet. Read books about finance, follow inspirational financial people on Instagram, such as @SuzeOrman and @thebudgetmom. Check to see how the money market works and how it trends. Become your own financial planner.

Make an Excel spreadsheet. Put all your expenses on one side and your income on the other side. Every time, keep the pattern of deducting your expenses from your income. It is a visual representation of finances.

I started my kids as soon as they started to learn how to count coins. In my household we still have the piggy bank system; whatever coins are laying around, we put in the piggy bank to save, and around Christmas, my kids can buy themselves something. They have saved all year long to treat themselves, and the boys enjoy it. They always looked forward to it. My goal was for my kids to understand the concept of saving.

I didn't have it all together when it came to finances in the beginning, and I would be a fake if

I pretended that I did. Neither my granny nor my mother was a good money manager. I was severely in debt with several credit card accounts open before I was even twenty years old. I was just swiping like nobody's business, buying stuff I didn't need (extra clothes, handbags, expensive shoes, nail shop visits faithfully every two weeks), and charging up my credit card like it was free money. Yes, I did go to a technical college and graduate, but nobody in school told me anything about how money works. From the ages of eighteen to twenty-seven, I was in the revolving cycle of spending more than I made. I was sick of it and needed to change my ways. All my credit cards had a high-interest rate, mistake number one. If I borrowed on a credit card of $1,000 with an interest rate of 24 percent, and I was making the monthly payment of $25, it made it nearly impossible to save. Just from this one credit card, the company made about $795 from interest. Let me remind you I had multiple cards, and saving money seemed impossible. And all the while I kept on wondering why it was so hard for me financially.

At the end of the day there was no excuse; clearly something was wrong. I acknowledged it. I knew I had to make it right, so I sought help with building up some self-discipline and a financial plan. As difficult as it was, I started to pay off all debts with any extra money I had, and that included my income taxes. I learned how to prioritize my spending habits. I was no longer going out to eat as often as I did before. My lifestyle changed in a real way. I viewed money differently. I kept a budget. I shopped with cash on hand instead of using my cards. It was refreshing giving the cashier at the stores exact change. That was new to me. My thoughts about money went from, "I've got it so I have to spend it," to "I have it; do I need to spend it?" I literally had to cut up all my credit cards, and within two years I was consumer debt-free.

In the beginning, it felt like a sacrifice. It was painful to me because I was not used to working with the details of my money. However, I had a vision to become debt-free, and that was bigger to me. Not to sound all preachy and stuff, I did trust and rely on God throughout the process. I prayed and meditated. My faith comes first knowing that the best was yet to come despite how the outer appearance looked. Being broke and in debt was temporary. I knew that much. What that looked like physically was that I purchased things with cash. I did meal prep to stretch my groceries longer. I stopped going to the nail shop as often. Basically, just because I had money did not mean I needed to spend it. If I didn't have what I wanted, I saved for it.

It takes time to find your rhythm. Every household is different, but practice and let faith do the rest.

OK, let's talk numbers. Think about it: $80 for every nail shop visit two times a week is $160, and there are fifty-two weeks in a year, which makes $8,320 was spent on nails with credit money that I did not have. Oh, yeah, don't forget the interest attached to that, and it was high. Another example is that I cut out eating at restaurants and fast food places. I saved about $200–300 a month while doing this. I took the time to prep meals and bought store-brand everything. Those pennies added up. After I taught myself some financial concepts, I became more confident because I could see that my bank account was not in the red. Consistency was the key.

Once you figure out how to save properly, you must figure out where to save your money and what types of accounts you should set up because a bank is the worst place you can put it. You hardly get any return on your money. I talked to many money coaches. I became a money coach. I studied the money-making rules so I could win the game. I read books like *Rich Dad Poor Dad*, by Robert Kiyosaki, and *You Are a Badass at Making Money*, by Jen Sincero. I listened to podcasts by Dave Ramsey and Suzie Orman. I wanted my finances to be better, so I did research. I took notes and applied them to my life once I learned my financial formula and noticed my weak spots. I ended my cycle of living paycheck to paycheck because I stopped myself from spending every dime I made. I was both saving and eliminating debt. It's a learning process that takes daily baby steps, staying consistent, and keeping your eyes on becoming debt-free.

3

Dating

Ladies, how you love plays a role in your destiny. It is 2020, and the dating scene has changed. Some men will still court you like the old days; it depends on what kind of guy you are entertaining. I find the single lifestyle is so peaceful. Many ladies get that mixed up with being lonely. Trust me, I am not. I am so involved with being a better version of myself that I date when I want to.

I am single, not celibate. I know how to get a man and keep a man based on his character. You must look for a man with integrity. Do his words match his actions? Does he have ambition? If you see a man lacking in an area where you feel unsafe or disrespected, just be single.

It's like this. Watch his actions. A man with good character will be ambitions, which means he will make money; therefore, he will pay bills and be a provider. That's the game; watch how he treats you while you date. I only had to experience one toxic relationship for me to get the game. I only needed to get played once. Yes, I admit that. But I haven't been played two times because I raised my standards and set some boundaries. I knew what I deserved, and I gained my self-worth. Build yourself up to the point you don't even attract players, liars, manipulators, or time wasters. I got that game quickly and told myself I would remain single until further notice. I just know I am not missing anything in the dating world. I am thankful that I am not settling for less than I deserve, which is a committed relationship that leads to marriage. If it doesn't happen, it's OK. I will be perfectly fine being a single mother.

I have been married before. To me, that's not the accomplishment; staying married is the accomplishment. I believe in dating with a purpose. That's the number one way to avoid unnecessary time in the relationship. Women of purpose just don't have time to entertain any man who's not up to par.

My dating tips and advice are not traditional. Neither do they go along with today's generational dating culture because I was raised by a gold-digging mother whose vice was to be with men because of what they could do for her financially. That's how a lot of women date. I will not tell a person who does not ask me what they should and should not do because I figure grown people are going to do what they want to do at the end of the day. I can only speak about my personal experience.

Normally, when I start to date, I simply ask myself if he is in alignment with my destiny now. Remember that vision you have for yourself and your kids, and keep that close to your heart. Depending on the man's character, you will be able to answer that question in time as you date. Also what qualities does he have, and how does he execute in his day to day activities. Ask him questions as you date, and watch for the follow-up. That is the part where ladies go wrong; a man can talk a good game, but actions speak louder than words with me and my kids.

If the man has kids or not, that's a personal preference, but the man must know that you have kids. There is no need to play mind tricks and beat around the bush about your kids. He must know up-front where he fits into your lifestyle. And if that's a deal-breaker for you, then he is not the one for you. Move on to the next. I would suggest dating men with children because it will always be a conversation starter and something you have in common. We are in a generation of heavily blended families. Don't get discouraged about this if you desire to have a man without kids. However, a man with kids will more easily see the relationship, and you can compare notes on how you both parent.

Side note, just because a man treats his children well does not mean he will treat yours well. I don't believe in competition with kids, and you will be surprised by how many women participate in games. Just make sure that it's not you. I often hear men with no kids tell me they would prefer women with no kids. I can see why. Think about it; a man has gone all this time in his life protecting himself by not having kids. So when he meets a woman with kids, it might be a deal-breaker.

When dating men with kids, keep in mind that the younger the child the more recent the relationship with the baby's mother. This can be negative or positive depending on the situation. Healthy communication is needed for coparenting but watch for the actions of both parents. Don't live in a state of paranoia, but be observant and see the signs of the relationship when dating a man with kids, especially during holidays. Make sure you are not the side chick.

What is your standard when it comes to blending families? That conversation with yourself has to be had. Some women don't mind the father spending the night over at the baby mother's house, whereas for some women that might be a trigger. I don't date men with kids under five years old because kids need their father around as much as possible during those years, and it's a deal-breaker if I find out a man has young children. I cut it off immediately. I won't put myself in the position to talk to a guy who should be focused on raising and spending time with his young children.

I've learned to be mindful of whom I sleep with; positive/negative sprits transfer from person to person, especially if he is not your husband. You can become attached and create a soul tie or an emotional connection with a man who is not your husband. In the meantime, limit sexual relationships. Just because you are dating a man does not mean you have to sleep with him. There is no pressure, ladies; you are in control when it comes to your body. Once you start to sleep with a man who is not your husband, emotions and feelings get in the way. You think it's love, but it's just infatuation and a soul tie. Let's save the heartbreak. You are looking for a man's character and integrity more from action than the words he speaks and rushing you to the bedroom is a red flag.

I remember dating this guy, and he was into spirituality heavily, but he was not practicing it in his life. Every time I would press him about it, he'd get annoyed. All he was talk. He really didn't have a road map he was following for his life, and I noticed that he was a people pleaser and didn't have a backbone. He would be like, "Trust is a process." However, he didn't have a track record long enough for me to follow, so I had to cut it off. I am not at that point to trust any man's process without action. Good conversation, but his execution was lacking, and that's one of my dating deal-breakers.

4

Single mom and business

No lie, you cannot half-step in this business area, ladies. This is how you make your money, so handle your business in every single way of the word. Having a business as a single mom and working a 9-to-5 job is two different sets of skills. The first is balance. It's 2020, and working forty hours a week for a company is not going to bring enough cash into the bank thanks to low wages. That's why I'm a strong advocate of women having a means of providing for themselves with multiple sources of income. Get creative and be marketable. Because everything is switching to online, start an online business. Think of something that can generate income. It can be either a product or service you are giving to people, and you are charging a fee for such things as watching kids, doing hair, tutoring, or selling T-shirts.

Start a small business; the goal is to work your way out of your 9-to-5 job. Depending on yourself for a paycheck is a scary thought because we all have been trained to work for someone else. However, did you know that deep inside you have hidden talents? Some people are not so fortunate as to have a support system. Sometimes people just have themselves and the grace of God. Trust yourself and the process. In the midst of making your coin, it's essential to make time for your kids, yourself, and work.

To do that, you must master the art of time management because it can be a lot to set a schedule. Break it into how many days a week you are going to spend in an area of your life. For example, Fridays and Sundays could be kid days and Saturday a self-care day. Then break it down into mornings or nights. Perhaps Friday nights and Sunday mornings and afternoons are for the kids, so plan how many hours for each activity.

I know my kids. They are getting bigger and really don't require as much time as before. I can get away with a movie on Friday night and on Sunday a fun day-trip to the park. Be flexible when you create a schedule; write your plans down; add them to your Google calendar, and incorporate them into your work and business activities through the rest of the week. If you are weak in the time management area, set a timer, and when it goes off, move on to the next task. Repeat this process, stay consistent, and watch how much you accomplish once you are focused.

I would like to touch on basic discipline. You must stick to whatever schedule and budget you have. If you have a specific deadline of 5 p.m., make sure you stick to it. Stay solid. In the end, that feeling of accomplishment can be addictive, and then you will be eager to start a new goal. At the end of the day, you will be extremely proud of yourself and how much you can accomplish in a certain amount of time. The next goal will be bigger and better. You get on the road to success by adding little changes in daily habits every day, repeating, and accomplishing. However, the household comes first. Try not to get so wrapped up in your business that you neglect finding your balance. This is key.

Before I stepped out and started up my finance business, I learned how to run my household first, meaning I would cook, clean, check homework, and go shopping until I could afford someone to do it for me. That was the goal. I am so thankful for Instacart; it has freed up time for me to work or tend to household needs because I have someone doing the shopping for me.

That's just an example of how to manage your time. This is the part most women struggle with. If you don't know what you are doing, it's hard to balance the weight of the household and work or run a business. Many women will get burned out. Some women will not pursue their goals because of their children; others work too much and neglect their kids. To be honest, I was all three of these types of mothers until I found my balance.

To help me, I did a survey of family and friends with about ten women. I asked what the one challenge they had as a single mother, and they all had a common answer: childcare. I get it; most women do not have someone they can trust to watch their kid as they pursue their dream, and I understand it. I remember that being a big issue for me as well until the boys turned five. I worked nights so I could be at home with my kids in the daytime so I didn't have an issue with childcare. I'm thankful for that, but I see how childcare can be an issue.

My kids were attached to my hip until they started school at five years old. We did everything together. However, now times have changed; many moms are working from home and creating online businesses. Back in the day, some single mothers had to coordinate with other single mothers a couple days a week to watch each other's kids day and night. I even know some mothers who can take their children to work with them. That's right, a corporate office with a daycare. Imagine that! When my boys were little, few people outside of childcare could watch them. I normally worked around their school schedules.

I found myself making lots of executive decisions. Sometimes I didn't have time to Google an answer or call someone for advice. Sometimes I had to think fast. For example, do I leave my kids home for an eight-hour shift because I was called in and I have no one else to watch them? Should I pay the water bill? I need gas in my car, and I can't afford to pay both this week. Every time I came across a situation like that I had to factor in my kids; how would this affect them? They need water, right? We must take baths. I had to think strategically, think business moves, so I would pay half of the water bill, make a payment arrangement, and see when it was due, hopefully by the next payday. I will pray I don't run out of gas for the week, or I might catch a ride from a co-worker who lives nearby. My point is problems/ troubles always have a solution.

I didn't take it personally, but I did hear the criticism. However, I didn't let it consume me. As you begin your journey for your new life, be prepared to be talked about and stay focused on your goal. Get to the point that your single mother game is so tight that no one can check you.

Ladies tend to get emotional, but you have to learn to put your emotions aside when dealing with people and your business. I learned that people don't care about your tears. They just want to see if they can make you cry. I am talking about the ones who mean you no good; let those haters be your motivators

5

Destiny over divorce

I wanted this to be the narrative of my life, and at first I wasn't going to talk about what made me a single mother, but I want to be transparent with my journey, so here it is. I was married to a childhood friend, and then I got divorced. The part many people don't know is that I left my husband, but we had dated for years. We met when

I was sixteen. He was a great man who didn't cheat, was not abusive, did no drugs, didn't lie, and gave me quality time. You see, he was a great man on the outside, but as I started to grow and mature, I felt that something was missing from the marriage. I continued to lie next to a man who was complacent and not ambitious and who didn't seem interested in personal change or going to the next level in life. He was not coachable. I had a problem with a man who could not execute as a provider. While we were dating, I did not see any of that. However, I wanted my destiny to be fulfilled. My taking care of a man, married or not, wasn't it.

We were unequally yoked; we were not aligned, but it took me about two years to figure it out. We just could not get it together; our personalities always clashed. We were opposites. I have always been bold, headstrong, outgoing, and loud in a certain environ-ment, and my ex-husband was the quiet type, very introverted, and didn't like to go out much. I had to push him out the door for date night.

I knew social environments made him uncomfortable, so I stopped asking him to go out with me and went out with my single friends instead. He said he loved me, but later I found out it was more like an emotional dependence. I took care of him as a woman. I made sure the rent was paid. I made sure we had food. I made sure he was doing well. I put him before myself, and I was over it. I should not have married a man without a job and with procrastination issues.

Yeah, I could have waited for him to catch up and put my destiny on pause, but that was difficult when I didn't see him put effort toward progress in the first place to better himself. I applied for jobs for him. I checked his email for his job interview status. I did all the leg work; all he had to do was show up to the interview. I would be so upset when he didn't get the job. I mean, damn. All he had to do was make a good impression and answer the questions, but I think he didn't want to work.

I mean, he was in denial about his depression at the time. We talked after the divorce, but it was already too late. I had already headed to Texas. I had had enough. I wanted out of the marriage, and I wanted my destiny. That was the reason for this book.

One thing about ambition: some people have it, and others don't. I always wanted the best out of life. I figured, why not reach for the stars? What's the worst that can happen?

But in my ex-husband's eyes, I was always doing too much. There is no other way to put it or say it; no one wants to be in a relationship with someone who doesn't have drive. That was important to me;

that was important for my kids to see an example of.

Now, single moms, you must follow through on your dreams and aspirations. If no one is going to help you, guess what? You have to help yourself. No one cares that you are a single mom. Stand strong with all the judgment that comes with not having a man in your home. You can either focus on that energy in a negative way and do nothing or in a positive way and let it push you to the next level in life. Stay focused; take the time to think about what you want to accomplish; put a time frame on it.

Execute! Do not stop until you reach the finish line; be an example for your children. Single mom, you have a purpose. Day by day, write your thoughts down and make them into a story to express all your emotions. Get details, paint a picture as you write, and do this until you feel that you have found your purpose in life. That's what I did.

I had to stop complaining. I wasn't perfect, and every statistic I was trying to avoid I became. I was a broken-home, single mother of two boys, divorced and living paycheck to paycheck, but what I can say is I did the work. I invested in myself and became more profitable.

6

Mind, body, and soul

There are levels to finding yourself, and sometimes you don't even have to dig deep. Just be aware of your feelings. If you are feeling overwhelmed with this process, it's OK. Don't rush. You will get there in time and find your peace of mind. Focus on what you can control, which are your thoughts, because your thoughts control your future. It all starts in your mind, and to change it must be renewed.

I know it sounds clichéd, but it is true. You must rise above every negative thought that comes to your mind; you have to rebuild yourself in a way that people from the old life won't recognize the new you.

In a sense, you have to deprogram yourself. Start with replacing negative thoughts with new positive thoughts. You have to fight that from within. Try to take "I hate" and "I can't" out of your vocabulary and replace them with "I am" and "I will." Make better decisions with the words that you speak. It's time for a change; change your eating habits if they are unhealthy. I don't have to be a nutritionist to say that when you eat good food, it gives your body proper energy and makes you feel better. It's all about becoming the best version of yourself. If you want better, put forth the action. You have to meal prep for the week, work out to get your body into the shape you desire, take care of yourself, love yourself, and keep your living quarters clean, not because you have to but because you want to.

Spend time with yourself alone. I promise your soul will thank you. Have spa days, walks around the park, movie time with yourself, and listen to a different genre of music. I listen to a lot of '90s R&B, but there's something about mediation music that takes me to a place mentally. It's very calming.

You are changing yourself from the past, which means the people around you will soon change. Just wait for that and adapt to the change because new people will gravitate toward you once you start to level up. That's one way to know you are moving in the right direction.

It's not a sprint but a marathon. I refused to settle. Yes, I was in a bad marriage; yes, I used to be taken advantage of. I used to work at a job that was not fulfilling to me or my destiny. Then I was fed up, and I changed because all the moves that I was doing were not working anymore. I knew it was time for me to go to the next level. I had been running from my calling for years by clubbing, working excessively, and ignoring the visions, thinking that the notion of my becoming a better individual would just go away, but nope.

I have been called to greatness. I noticed nothing was going right within my own will. I could not save money; I was gaining weight; I was not investing in myself mind, body, or soul. I was not taking the time to get to know me until I hit rock bottom, and then I surrendered.

You see, this book is for single moms who are creating the life they want for their kids despite their past situations. This book is for women who outgrew the hot-girl summers and want more out of life and just need someone to relate to. It's also for single moms who need to know more about how to overcome adversity. Finally, this book is for single moms who understand that life is not hopeless.

You are a single mom by accident; you have some struggles and some testimony as well so that you can help the next single mother get through. So, single mom, I challenge you to now go and write your own story.

"Always concentrate on how far you have come, rather than how far you have left to go. The difference is how easy it seems will amaze you."—**Heidi Johnson**

ABOUT THE AUTHOR

Andrea Watson is a single mother of two boys and a business owner with a background in health care and finance. She is determined to be the best mother to her boys. In her book, *Single Mother for the Win*, she gives her personal advice on how to get through life's struggles while being a single mother. In her words, "No matter what you go through, be brave just like a rose from the concrete, and make something out of yourself."

She is from San Diego and now resides in Austin, Texas.